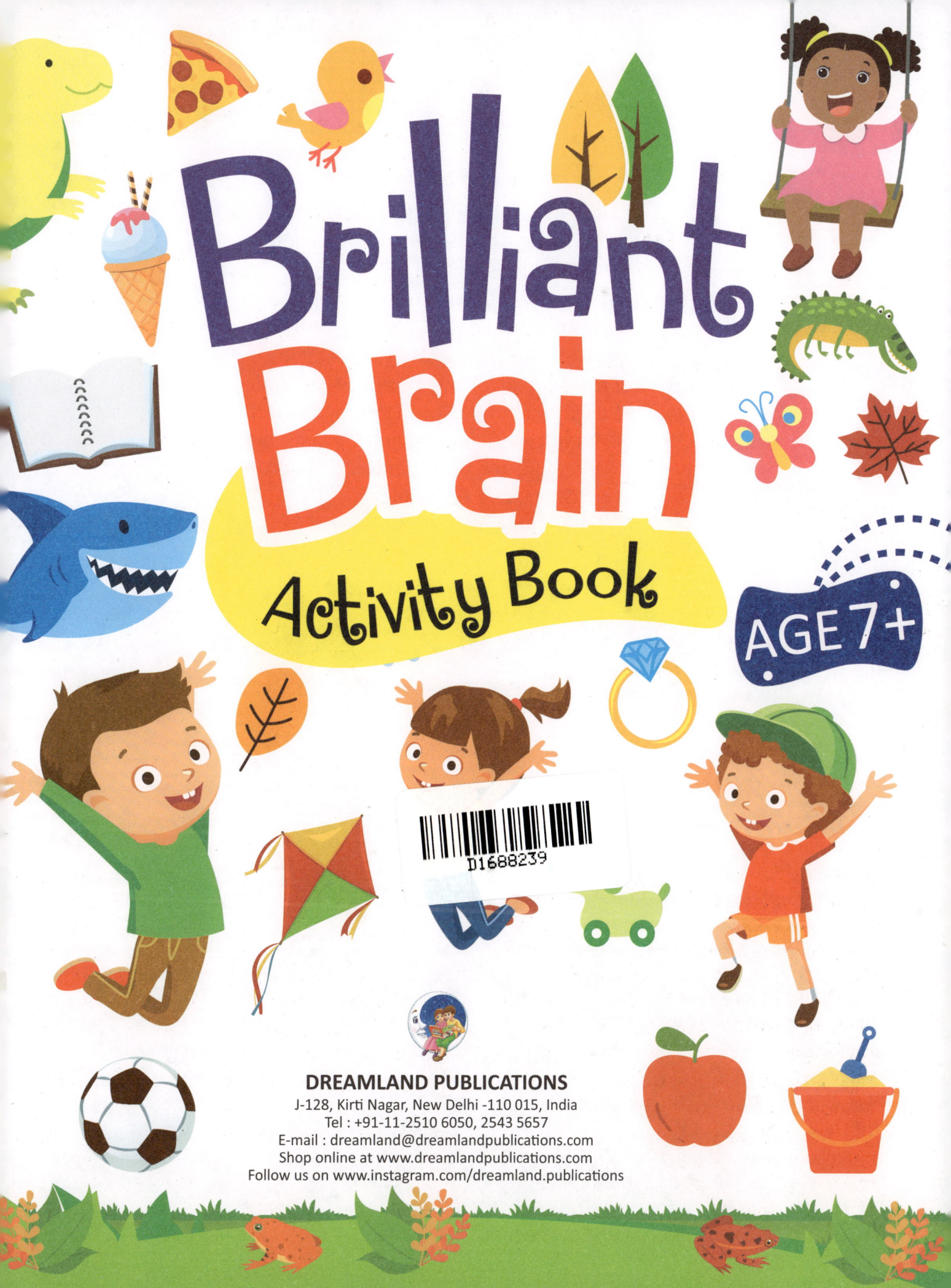

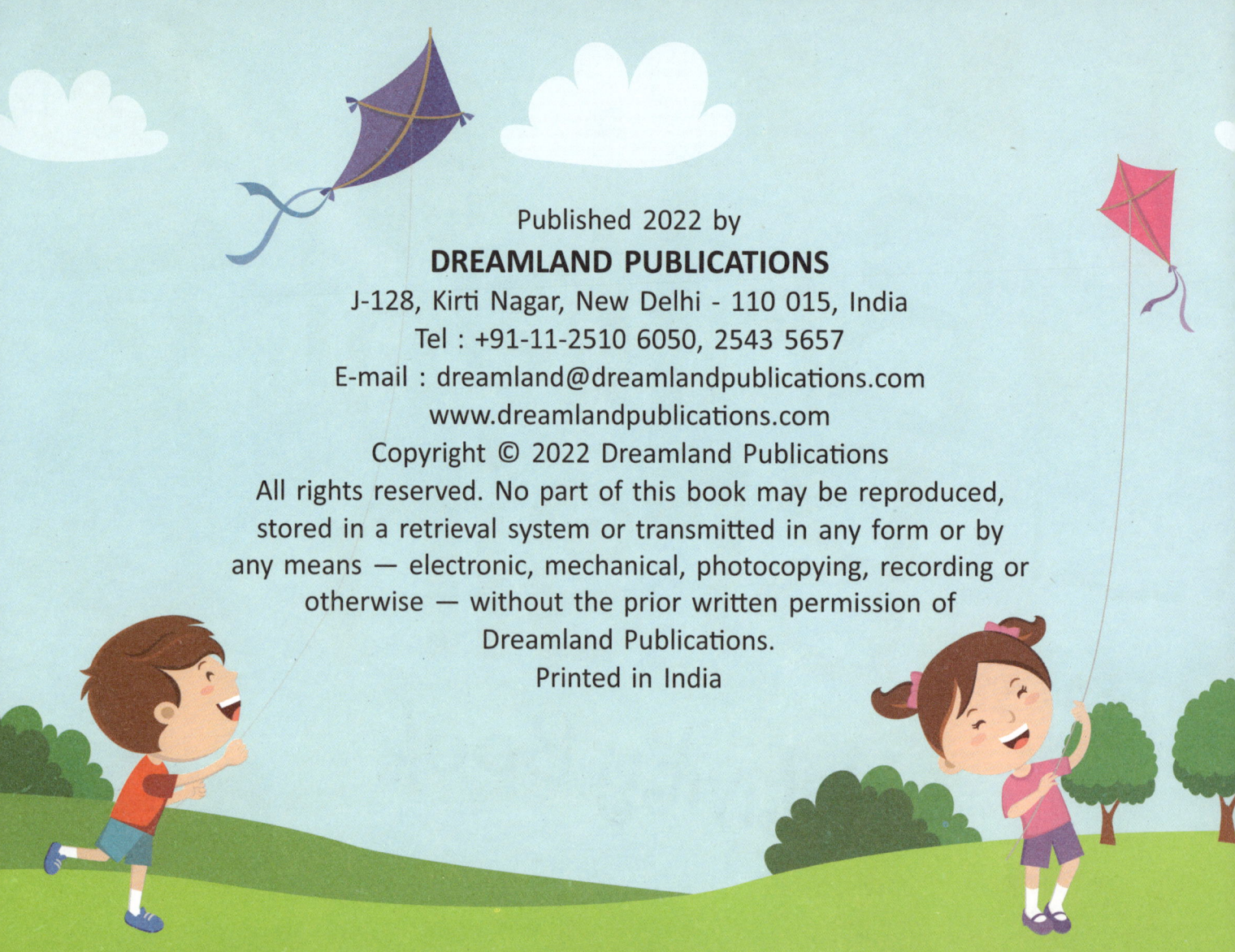

Published 2022 by
DREAMLAND PUBLICATIONS
J-128, Kirti Nagar, New Delhi - 110 015, India
Tel : +91-11-2510 6050, 2543 5657
E-mail : dreamland@dreamlandpublications.com
www.dreamlandpublications.com
Copyright © 2022 Dreamland Publications
All rights reserved. No part of this book may be reproduced, stored in a retrieval system or transmitted in any form or by any means — electronic, mechanical, photocopying, recording or otherwise — without the prior written permission of Dreamland Publications.
Printed in India

Preface

We are hardwired to learn. And fortunately or unfortunately, 'early learning' does not happen in chunks. As parents or educators, we would prefer if numbers are about 'Math' and experiments are about 'Science'.

But something brilliant happens when different areas of learning are connected and children receive knowledge and experience life as a whole. To put it more simply, the more children are taught to 'connect the dots' in real life; the more neural pathways are formed within the brain. And what does that mean?

That means a smarter child, who is well adapted and 'primed' for cognitive abilities.

This series of short mental exercises will help children to make new neural pathways and have fun with child–centric themes.

The aim of the book is to not just 'finish' it. Remember, activities and exercises supplement intelligent conversations - which is where you, as a parent, caretaker or teacher, become a part of the process and of this book.

The hope of this fresh series from Dreamland is to not just keep your child engaged but gainfully and creatively enjoy the learning process.

1. 'Send' and 'Receive' are antonyms. Tick the answer.

a) TRUE

b) FALSE

2. Cross the shape that is ¾ coloured.

3. Tick to show which of the following has **kinetic** (object in motion) energy?

4. **Polar regions** are very far away from the **equator**, so they are very _____.
Write the answer in the blank.

a) hot

b) cold

c) wet

d) dry

5. Fill in the blank with a word from the options given below.

The girl ran around the _____ playground.

a) thin   b) thick   c) large   d) high

6. Draw to show 12:35 on the clock.

7. All plants and animals are _____ organisms. Circle the correct answer.

a) large   b) living
c) non-living   d) breathing

8. Tick the word that is used to name a fruit and a colour.

a) RED   b) PLUM   c) YELLOW   d) GREEN

9. The chessboard consists of squares arranged in two alternating colours (light and dark). Tick the option that is TRUE.

a) There are 32 light squares. ☐

b) There are 30 light squares. ☐

c) There are 28 dark squares. ☐

d) There are 34 dark squares. ☐

10. Fill in the blank with the correct article.

_____ little girl with a ponytail is eating an apple.

11. Circle the amphibian.

12. Cross the odd one in the series.

13. Rewrite the sentence by capitalizing the correct words.

jane scored higher than sam.
_____

14. Draw the equator line on this image with red broken lines.

15. How many poles does Earth have? Circle the answer.

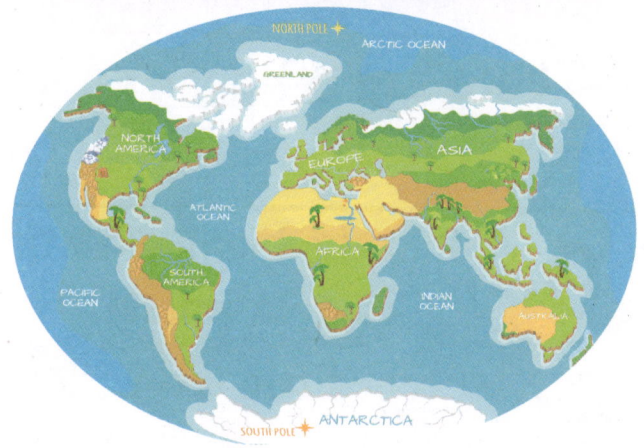

1   **2**   **3**   **4**

16. What are papers made of? Circle the correct picture.

17. Add 'the' where required.

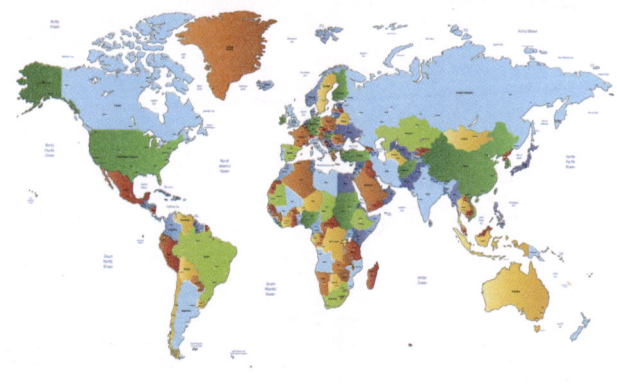

1. ____ USA   2. ____ Australia

3. ____ UAE   4. ____ Africa

18. Fill in the blanks with the correct punctuations.

Wow __ we did it __   ! ? . ,

19. Order the words alphabetically.

1. hour   2. horror   3. honest   4. hope   5. hoot   6. hollow

___ -> ___ -> ___ -> ___ -> ___ -> ___

20. Circle the female of a peacock.

21. Circle the person from the Orient (countries of the Far East).

22. Circle the correct option to fill both the blanks.

The Earth takes _____ to rotate on its ____.

- A. 12 hours, axis
- B. 24 minutes, axis
- C. 24 hours, pole
- D. 24 hours, axis

23. Cross the picture that ends with 'g'.

24. What time will the clock show after 10 minutes? Tick the correct option.

a) 10 past 1   b) 10 to 1
c) 10 to 12   d) 10 past 12

25. Circle to show the home of a caterpillar before it becomes a butterfly?

26. What can a mixer grind? Cross the correct option.

27. Tick that which can help to produce electricity.

28. Fill in the correct ordinal number.

The ____ apple is outside the box.

29. Circle the organs that are part of the digestive system.

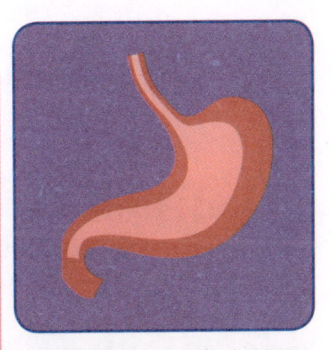
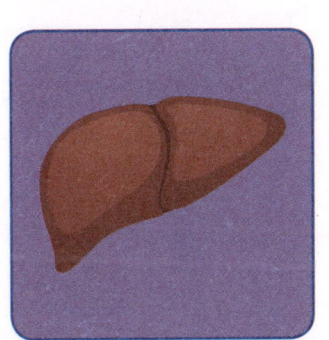
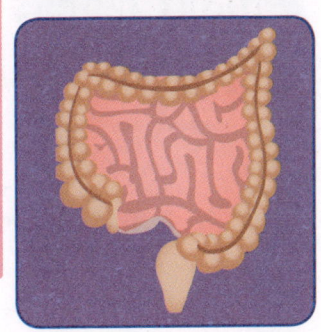
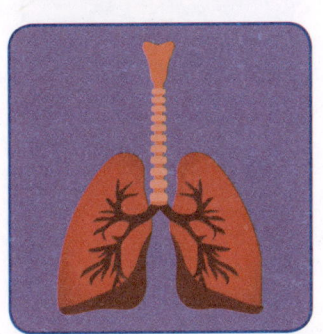

30. Cross the box that is crimson.

31. Did you know? Dolphins breathe through lungs!

Colour the dolphin.

32. Fill in the blank with the correct word from the options given below.

I ate _____ banana this morning.

a) a   b) an   c) the   d) some

33. How many blocks does the penguin need to cross to reach the ice box? Circle the answer.

13   14   12   8

34. Match the organs with the system they belong to.

   skeletal

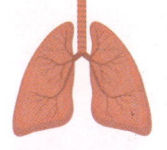   digestive

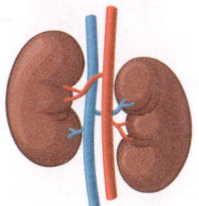   respiratory

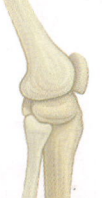   excretory

35. Circle the decomposer of a food chain.

36. Tick the country names that are preceded by 'the'.

- ☐ United Kingdom
- ☐ Netherlands
- ☐ United Arab Emirates
- ☐ United States of America

37. Without calculating, put a tick for the numbers that are divisible by both 2 and 5.

a) 1560 _____

b) 27895 _____

c) 569430 _____

d) 1784228 _____

38. Tick the option that the arrow is pointing at.

- FLOWER ☐
- STEM ☐
- ROOTS ☐
- LEAF ☐

39. Which of these are also called the 'building blocks of life'? Circle the picture.

Cells

Leaves

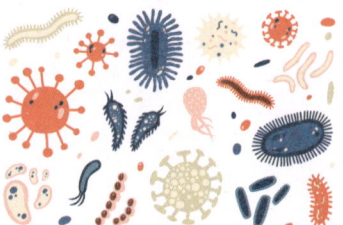
Microorganisms

Sun

40. Spot and circle 5 differences.

41. Write the past tense of each 'irregular verb'.

think	
am	
beat	
wake	
burst	
forbid	

42. Tick the answer.

John has 16 sheep.
He wants to divide them equally in 4 groups.
How many sheep does he keep with himself?

a) 1   b) 3   c) 2   d) 0

43. Circle the fish that are 'mammal'.

44. Tick the duration Earth takes to complete one revolution around the sun.

a) 365 days

b) 367 days

c) 368 days

d) 370 days

45. Circle the mirror image of this shape: ★

46. Which picture shows LUNAR eclipse? Tick the correct picture.

47. Excessive of which rays of the Sun is harmful for us? Cross in the box next to it.

1. infrared

2. ultraviolet

48. Circle the objects that are *portable*.

49. What is the opposite of North-West? Cross the correct option.

a) NORTH-EAST   b) SOUTH-EAST

c) WEST   d) SOUTH-WEST

50. What causes high waves in the seas at night? Cross the picture.

Sun Moon
Saturn Earth

51. Circle the picture that shows a 'communicable' disease.

52. Circle the 'octagon'.

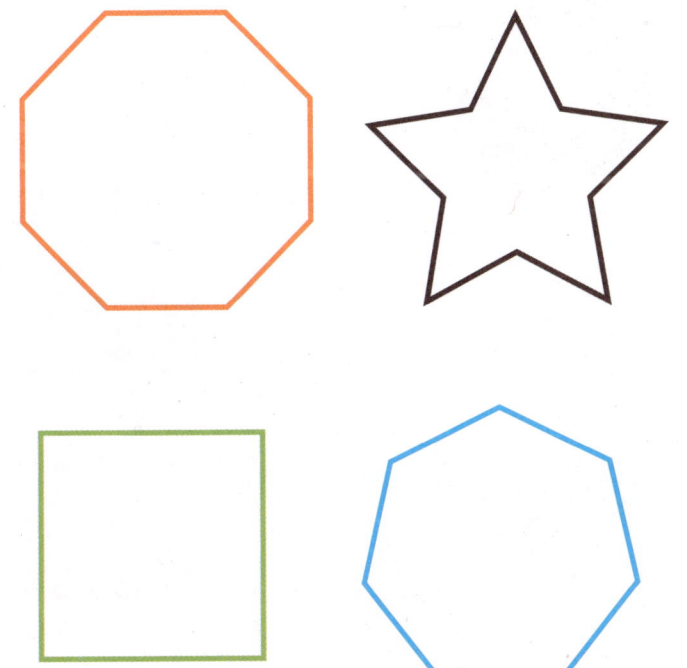

53. Tick the name of the body part inside which your lungs are.

A. Head

B. Stomach

C. Chest

D. Legs

54. Circle the vegetables that have starch.

55. Complete and colour the pictures.

56. What is a group of bees called? Tick it.

A. Herd

B. Group

C. Swarm

D. Bunch

57. Match parts of our natural environment with the correct picture.

A

lithosphere

B

biosphere

C

hydrosphere

D

atmosphere

58. What gives leaves their green colour?

C _ _ O _ _ _ H _ LL

59. Circle the object that has mechanical (machine) energy.

60. Which nutrient do we get from the sun? Circle it.

1. Calcium
2. Mineral salts
3. Vitamin D
4. Vitamin B

61. Fill in the boxes with the correct numbers.

A. 70 = ___ tens + ___ ones

B. 56 = ___ tens + ___ ones

C. 3 = ___ tens + 3 ones

D. ___ = 1 tens + 1 ones

62. Circle the animal that is a **vertebrate** (that has backbone).

63. What kind of force does 'gravity' put on everything on Earth? Tick the answer.

64. Which vegetable is a root? Circle your answer.

65. Circle the correct **consonant blend** to fill the blank.

_____ ane

a) pl b) gr

c) cl d) sm

66. What is half of a circle called? Write in the blank.

67. What is the 3D figure of a rectangle called? Cross the answer.

1. cube

2. sphere

3. cone

4. cuboid

68. Tick the statements that tell you how to be a good citizen.

a) When you go for picnic, you clean up the place after you are done.

b) If your classmate does not agree with you, you get into a fight with him.

c) You do not help an elderly person cross the road.

d) You are polite with your neighbours.

69. Tick the correct spelling according to the picture.

plane/plain

dear/deer

write/right

two/too

70. Fill in the blank with the correct **numerator**.

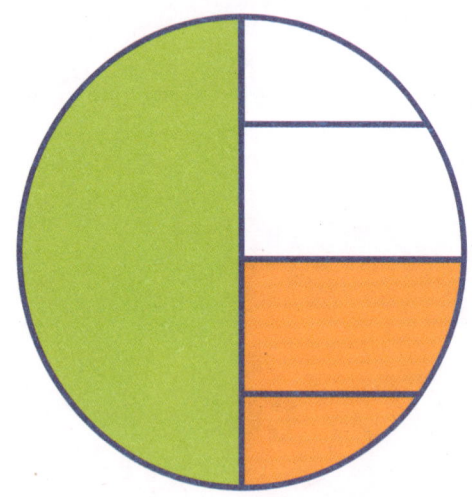

1/2 = ___/4

71. What do the tree and the elephant have in common? Spell it out.

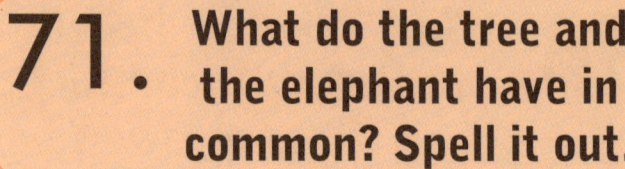

_ _ _ _ _ _ _

72. Do you know the **chemical names** of these things? Give it a try.

water = ___

carbon dioxide = ___

oxygen = ___

ozone = ___

73. Circle the pictures of which we can find the volume.

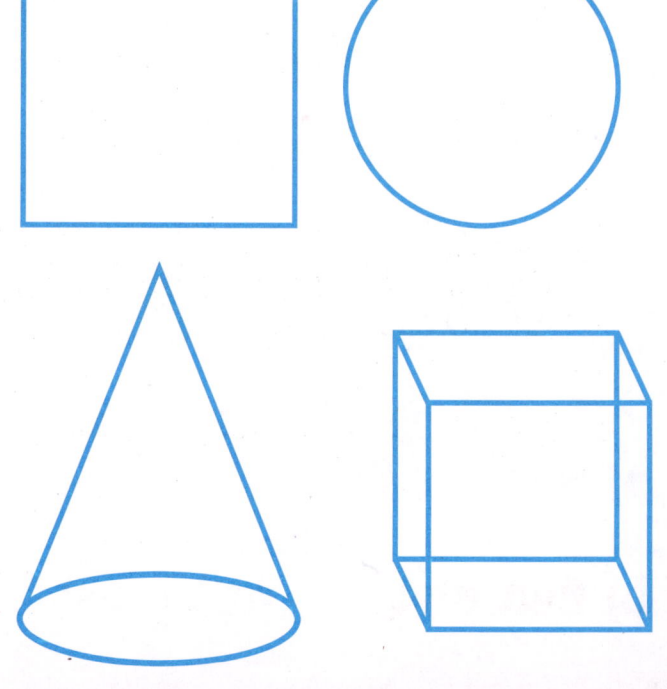

74. At what temperature does water become ice? Tick the answer.

A. 0°C ☐

B. 100°C ☐

C. 20°C ☐

D. 5°C ☐

75. Complete the conversion equations.

1 m = ___ cm

1 kg = ___ g

1 l = ___ ml

1 byte = ___ bits

1 MB = ___ KB

76. Which layer of soil is at the lowest level?

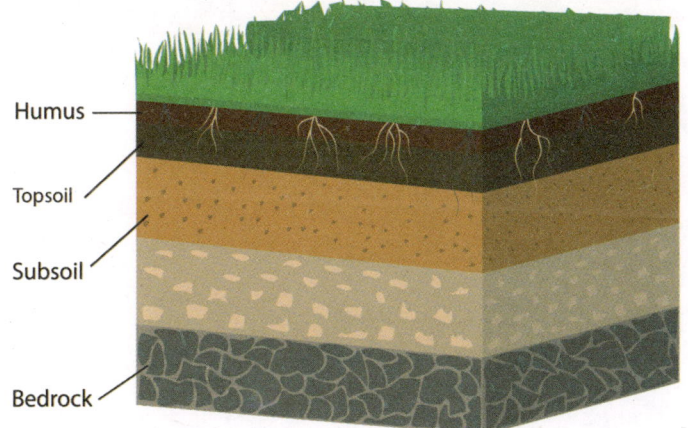

a) Subsoil   b) Humus

c) Bedrock   d) Topsoil

77. Circle the place that is a country as well as a continent.

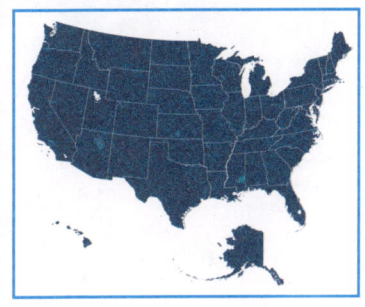 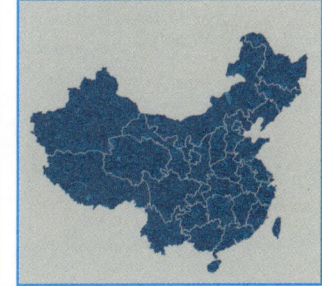

21

78. Which fish is known to produce electric current? Circle it.

79. Tick the sentences that have a wrong punctuation mark.

a) May I come in? ○

b) Wow! This is beautiful! ○

c) Do you mind sharing! ○

d) His name is Rod. ○

80. Solve the division problems.

15 ÷ 5 = _____

____ ÷ 4 = 4

81. When ice melts, it turns into steam. Tick the answer.

TRUE ◯   FALSE ◯

82. Circle the process of evaporation, cross condensation and tick precipitation.

83. The standard room temperature is 24°C. True or False?

TRUE ◯   FALSE ◯

84. Choose the right option to fill the blank.

My teacher _____ me to get down from the bus yesterday.

A. helping ☐
B. helps ☐
C. helped ☐
D. help ☐

85. Figure out the number pattern and fill the empty coaches of the train.

86. Fill in the blanks with the correct verbs.

1. They ____ (goes / go) to the fair every year.

2. I ____ (need / needs) to practise Math more.

3. Joshua ____ (want / wants) a toy robot as his next birthday gift.

4. People everywhere ____ (wishes / wish) only for peace.

87. Cross the picture that shows one of the Seven Wonders of the World.

88. Put a tick mark for the correct adverb types.

- Adverb of place
- Adverb of manner
- Adverb of agent
- Adverb of direction

89. Circle the picture of the word that has the short 'a' sound in it.

90. How many hands are there in the picture? Tick the right number.

| 5 | 2 | 3 | 4 |

91. Circle the 'beasts of burden'.

92. Which statements make this number? 125

- 100 + 25
- 100 + 52
- 130 − 15
- 150 − 25

93. Connect the dots to see which animal it is.

94. Tick the plural word of cactus.

A. cactuses

B. cact

C. cactoes

D. cacti ✓

95. Circle the living thing that produces its own food.

96. Cross that which is 'no longer' part of our solar system.

97. Cross the odd one out.

98. Tick the correct word according to the picture.

A. balling ☐
B. boiling ☐
C. bolling ☐
D. bowling ☐

99. How many shapes are there in this picture? Tick the right option.

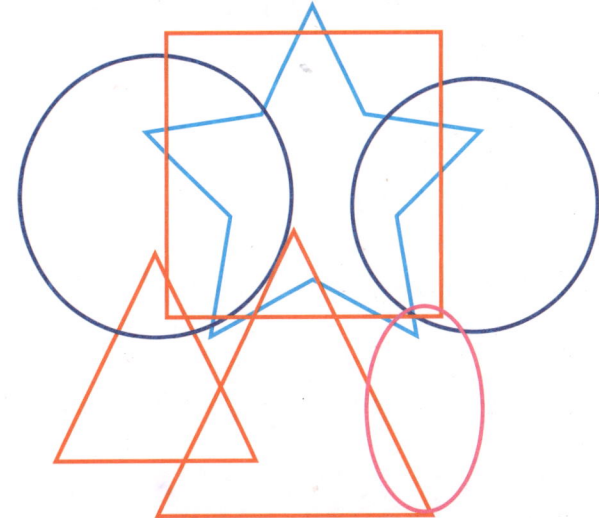

5   6   7   8

100. Cross the parasite.

101. Which is the fastest mode of transportation? Circle and show.

102. How many beans? Tick the right option.

Anna has 26 jellybeans. She wanted to give half of them to Bob. She gave 14 to Bob. Is the number correct?

a) No, Bob received more.

b) Yes, Bob received the correct number.

c) No, Anna had more.

d) Anna did not give anything to Bob.

103. Is the boy following traffic rules? Tick the right answer.

YES   NO

104. Write the given times in the 12-hour format. The first one is done for you.

1. 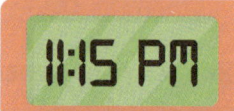 11:15 PM

2.

3.

4.

105. Circle the objects before which we always use 'a pair of'.

106. What colour do you get when you mix **Blue** and **Red**? Tick the right answer.

A. Magenta ☐
B. Purple ☐
C. Yellow ☐
D. Orange ☐

107. If tomorrow is Monday, what day was day before yesterday? Tick and show.

A. Tuesday ☐
B. Saturday ☐
C. Sunday ☐
D. Friday ☐

108. Circle the word that is a **synonym** of the word 'grumpy'.

A. joyful
B. stressed
C. angry
D. surprised

109. 6 apples cost $10. 5 oranges cost $8. If Jane bought 12 apples and 10 oranges, how much did it cost her in total? Tick the right answer.

$26 $40

$18 $36

110. Which is the second layer of the earth from the top? Tick the right answer.

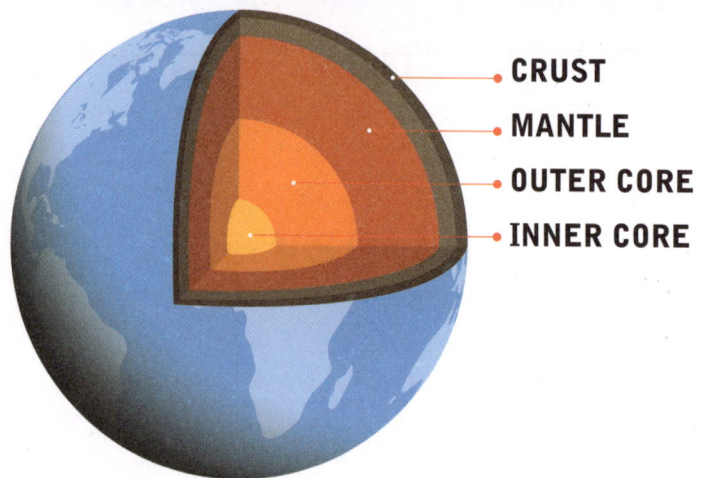

A) mantle ☐   c) crust ☐

b) inner core ☐   d) outer core ☐

111. Circle the natural resources.

112. Circle the picture that has the shape of a cylinder.

113. Choose the correct consonant blend and complete the word.

_____ ack.

a) cr   b) pr

c) dr   d) fr

114. What fraction of these animals are **not** dogs? Circle the right answer.

a) 3/5 b) 2/5 c) 1/5 d) 4/5

115. Circle the tree that you can expect to see in the mountainous region.

116. Which country is the closest to the North Pole? Tick the right answer.

A. England
B. Greenland
C. Iceland
D. Canada

117. How many balls are touching the vase? Circle the right number.

21
15
17
16

118. Tick and tell what or who is the subject (what or who the sentence is talking about) of the sentence.

Haley sat down at her computer to work.

a) Haley ○ b) Her ○

c) Down ○ d) Computer ○

119. How many blocks away is the boy from the house? Circle the right number.

10   9   14   11

2 3 4 5 6 7 8 9 10 11 12 13 14

120. Circle the objects that are non-metals.

121. Circle and show which of these you would find in a museum.

122. Which two consecutive months have 31 days? Tick the pair.

1. July and August

2. September and October

3. March and April

4. November and December

123. Find and circle the names of the given organisms in the word search.

M	O	S	Q	U	I	T	O	A
A	H	G	S	T	P	A	B	C
S	O	L	I	Z	A	R	D	C
D	N	J	S	D	R	D	U	Q
F	E	K	R	Q	C	Y	N	M
G	Y	L	Q	R	G	H	P	B
P	B	T	P	T	B	V	N	T
Q	E	Y	D	Y	Q	U	R	S
R	E	M	N	G	T	B	D	J
B	U	T	T	E	R	F	L	Y

124. Fill in the blanks with the correct symbol (greater than, less than or equal to).

A. 12 ☐ 15

B. 10 ☐ 8

C. 20 ☐ 20

D. 23 ☐ 23

125. Cross to show which bird lays the largest egg.

126. Circle the planet that has the largest number of moons.

Earth   Saturn
Neptune   Jupiter

127. Cross the shape that is NOT a *polygon*.

128. Unscramble the letters to show what's in the picture.

C S O T N I T N E N =

_____

129. Which two shapes share the longest border? Tick the correct answer.

A. B and C ☐

B. C and D ☐

C. A and B ☐

D. All the shapes ☐

130. Circle the fastest animal.

131. Walking is one form of transportation. Circle the answer.

YES
NO

132. What is the correct way of writing the hour before 1:00 pm? Tick the right answer.

A. 12:00 am ☐
B. 12 noon ☐
C. 12:00 pm ☐
D. 12 midnight ☐

133. Fact or Opinion? Circle the right answer for the given statements.

1. Lunch hour starts at noon.

Fact   Opinion

2. The sun is the largest body in the solar system.

Fact   Opinion

134. Cross the rabbits with the lowest value.

A: 4 x 2 B: 4 + 2 C: 4 – 2 D: 4 / 2

135. Sound is energy that travels by air and is caused by _____.
Fill in the correct word to complete the fact.

friction   decibels   matter   vibrations

136. What is the latitude at 23°27' N of the Equator called? Tick your answer.

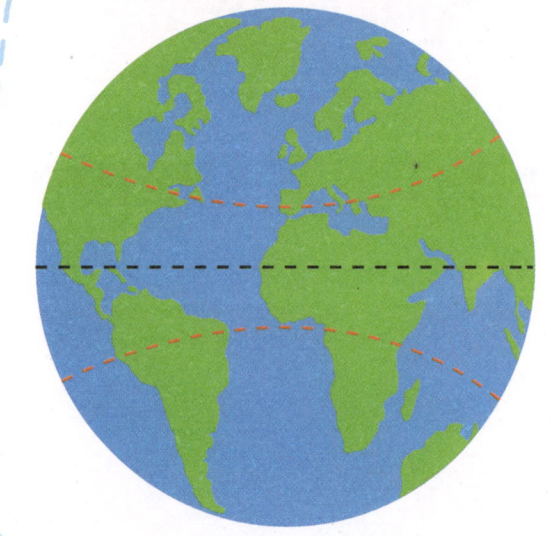

a. Tropic of Cancer ○
b. Tropic of Capricorn ○

137. Circle the mirror image of this picture.

138. Cross the objects that can protect you from an electric shock.

139. How many colours do you see? Draw a line from the cube to the right number.

6   26   27   10

140. Cross the body part that is infected when you have cough.

141. You are a teenager from age 13 to 19. True or False?

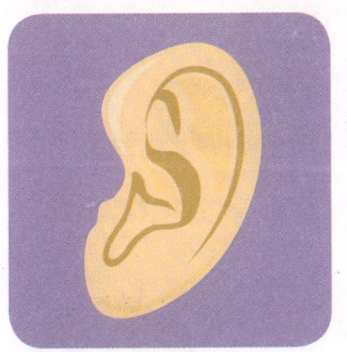

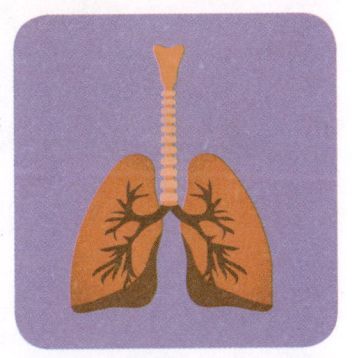

TRUE   FALSE

142. How many corners does this shape have? Circle the right answer.

A 5
B 4
C 6
D 7

143. Fill in the blank to complete the sentence.

_____ saves us from slipping.

a. Friction   b. Motion   c. Sound   d. Force

144.
Line D is higher than line B by how many units? Circle the right answer.

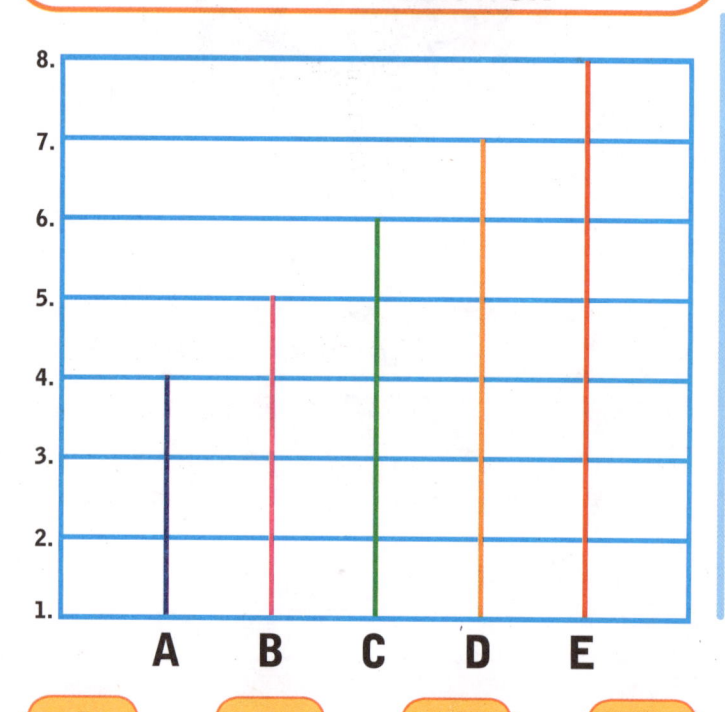

3   4   5   2

145.
The melted material that flows out of a volcano is called _____.

Choose the correct option to fill in the blank.

silver   lava   fire   mercury

146.
Which of these is the most abundant element in the Earth's crust? Tick the correct answer.

A. Carbon   B. Nitrogen

C. Hydrogen   D. Oxygen

147. What is missing in this picture? Circle and show from the options given.

- Tail
- Ears
- Nose
- Hair

148. Circle all the vowels in the given words. Also, write in the box the vowel(s) you could not find here.

A P P L E

C H E E T A H

U M B R E L L A

A V A C A D O

149. Which digit in this number is in the hundreds place? Cross it.

2 0 1 9

150. Circle the animal that is an omnivore.

151. Which is the most abundant metal in the Earth's crust. Cross the answer.

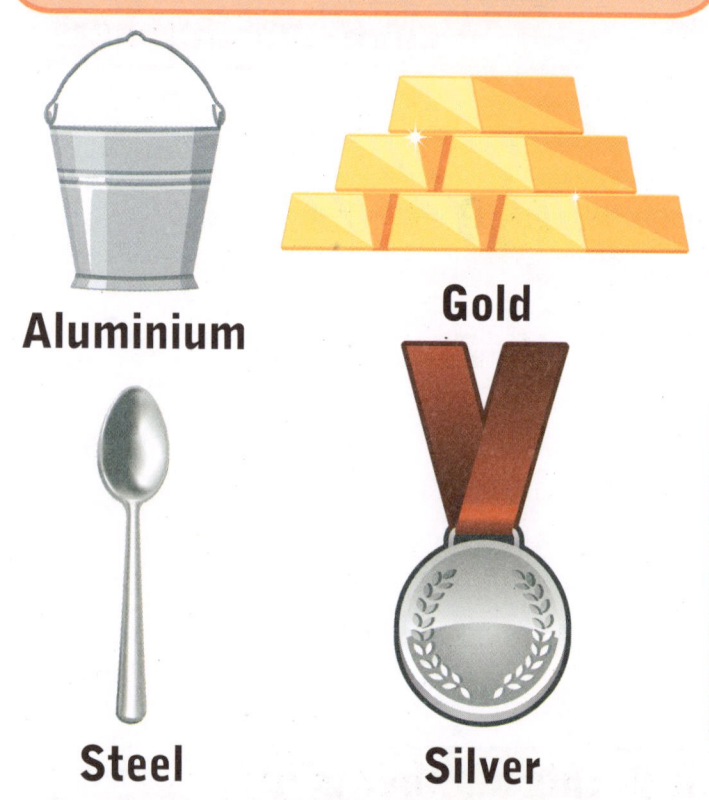

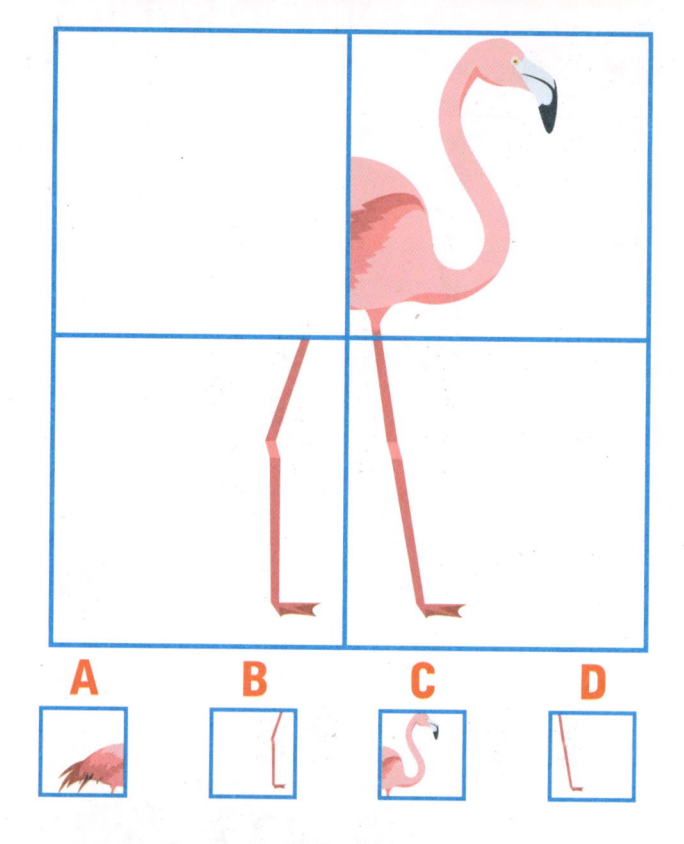

Aluminium

Gold

Steel

Silver

152. Choose and circle the missing piece of the puzzle.

A B C D

153. Circle the planet that is the farthest from the Sun.

Earth

Saturn

Mars

Neptune

154. Circle the shape that is coloured 1/4th.

155. Which bird do you see at night? Circle the picture.

156. What colour is closest to the Magenta colour? Tick the right option.

A. Blue
B. Green
C. Yellow
D. Red

157. Which is the next figure in the series? Circle the right option.

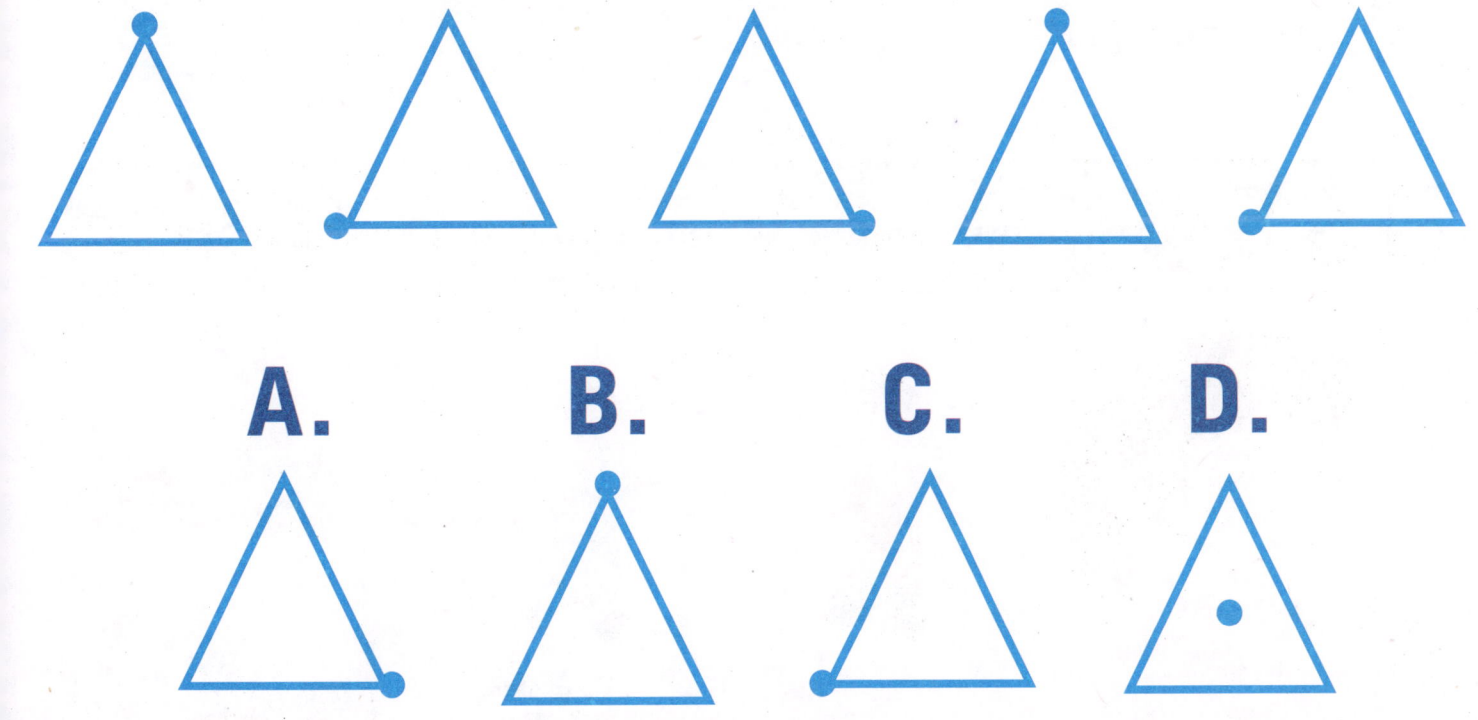

A.　　B.　　C.　　D.

158. Add 'es' or 's' at the end of the words to make them plural.

A. ball _____   B. tabl _____

C. pencil _____   D. candl _____

159. Which shape has no corners? Tick the right answer.

A. Square ☐

B. Triangle ☐

C. Oval ☐

D. Pentagon ☐

160. Tick the place that will have the most rainfall.

161. Which habit is good to begin your day in the morning?

162. If you bought 5.5 metres of a cloth piece, how many centimetres of cloth did you buy?

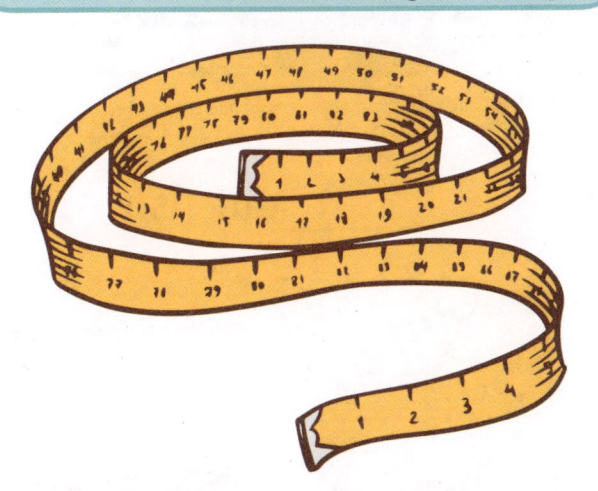

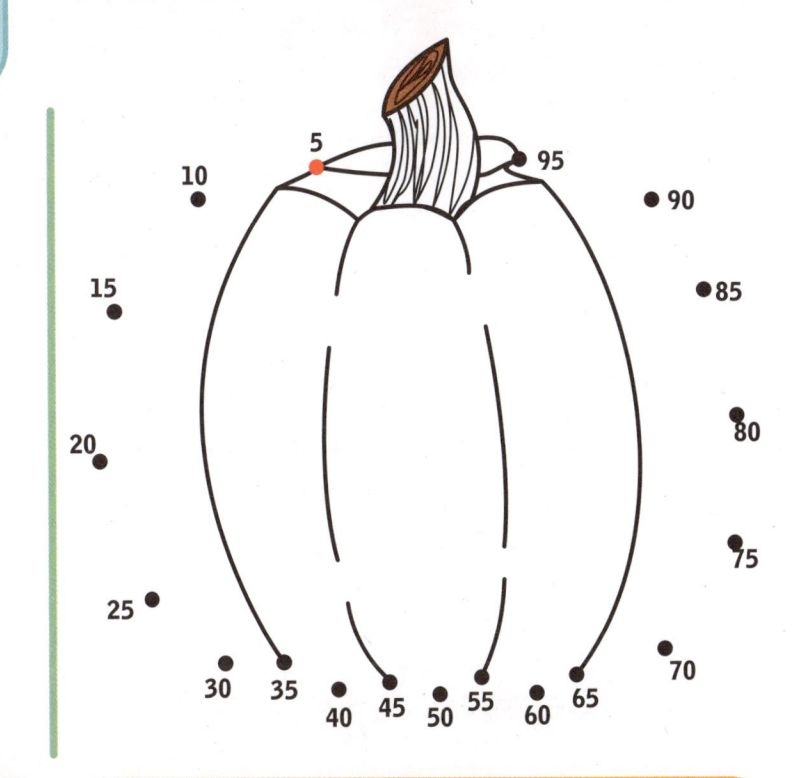

a. 550 cm
b. 515 cm
c. 55 cm
d. 5.5 cm

163. Join the dots on **multiples** of 5 to complete the picture.

164. Tick the name of the insect that produces a material for clothes.

A. Butterfly
B. Silkworm
C. Spider
D. Earthworm

165. Circle the food item that has the nutrient to make our teeth stronger.

166. Tick the tenth month of the year from the options below.

A. January ☐
B. December ☐
C. November ☐
D. October ☐

167. What is a group of these animals called? Write in the blanks given.

a _____ of fish

a _____ of bees

168. What would you get if you evaporate sea water? Circle the correct answer.

a. nothing
b. salt
c. sugar
d. shells

169. _____ living things need water to survive. Cross the right answer.

A. All
B. Few
C. Non-
D. Many

170. What does the water turn into in the water cycle? Circle the answer.

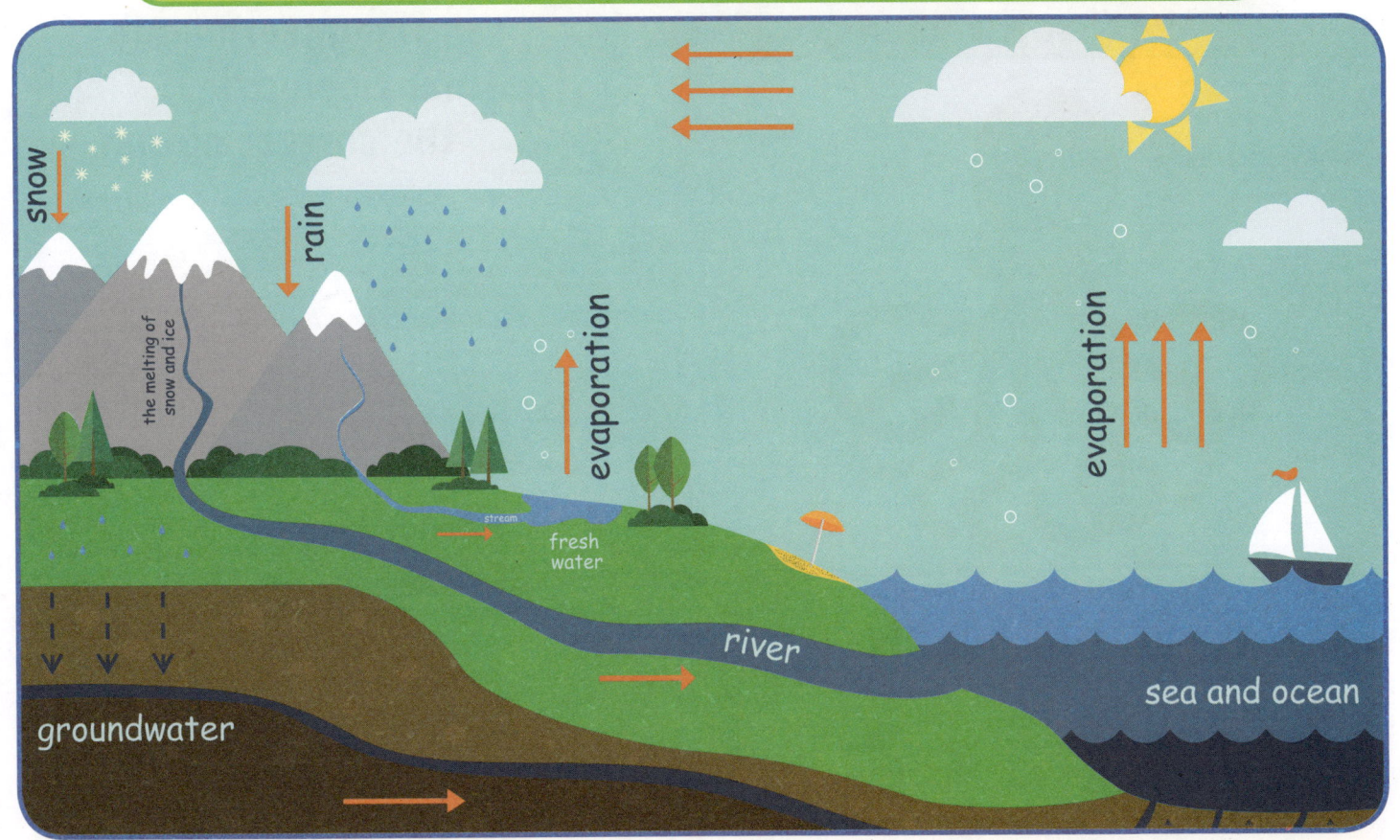

Land   Clouds   Sun   Oceans

171. Help the turtle find its way to the apple.

172. My teacher, Mrs Hannigan, is very nice. She helps me solve my math problems very easily.

Tick to show what topic the statement above is about.

A. A football game ○   B. Mrs Hannigan ○

C. Mathematics ○   D. Me ○

173. What number does 'octo' in octopus mean? Tick the answer.

a. 8   b. 6
c. 4   d. 2

174. Who out of these is at the highest position in the government of many countries? Tick the correct option.

A. President
B. Principal
C. Parents
D. Minister

175. How many triangles are there? Tick the right answer.

A. 5   B. 4
C. 3   D. 6

176. Another word for smart is foolish. Circle the right answer.

TRUE   FALSE

177. Harry divides his 40 books in sets of 5. How many sets does he create? Circle the answer.

A. 10   B. 8
C. 6   D. 4

178. Circle the vegetables that can be eaten **raw**.

179. What colours will you mix to get orange? Tick the right answer.

A. Red and Blue ☐

B. Red and Yellow ☐

C. Blue and Yellow ☐

D. Red and Green ☐

180. Solve the Sudoku.

181. My math book is _____ than my geography book.

A. big ☐

B. bigger ☐

C. biggest ☐

D. best ☐

	4	3	2	7		1		
2	1	7	9		5		4	3
3							2	7
	3	1				4		8
5	9			4	3	2		
	7		6	5	8	1	3	
	4		2	3				
	5	6		7	4	3		2
8		3		1		7	6	4

182. How many squares are shaded? Tick the right answer.

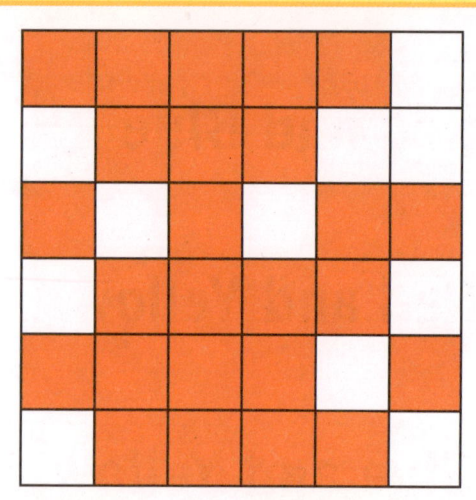

A. 20 B. 25
C. 30 D. 35

183. Circle the plant that is a carnivore.

184. Circle the items that one 'wants'.

185. Cross the odd one out.

48

186. Write 'un' or 'dis' and complete the words.

A. _____ derwear

B. _____ appointed

C. _____ tie

D. _____ approved

187. Which is the heaviest?

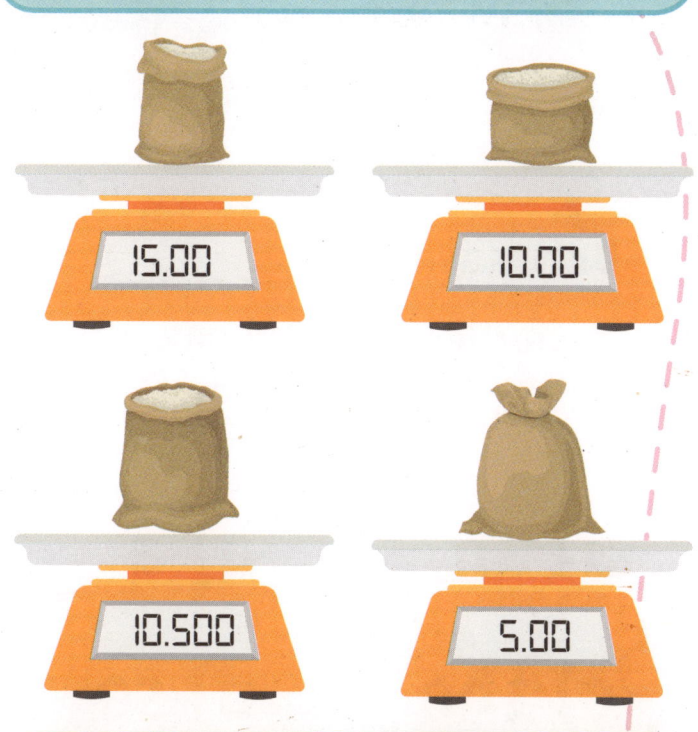

15.00   10.00

10.500   5.00

188. Circle the place where ants live.

189. A constellation is a group of stars that form an imaginary shape like an animal or creature. Tick the right answer.

TRUE ☐   FALSE ☐

190. Circle to show which animal is the fourth from left in the two rows.

191. Fill in the blank with the correct article from the options given below.

Only Kevin had _____ superhero comic book in the whole school.

a) an   b) a
c) the d) so

192. Tick the equation that has all the numbers in tens.

A. 31 + 10 − 40
B. 25 + 25 − 0
C. 33 + 20 − 10
D. 10 + 20 + 10

193. Photosynthesis takes place during the day as well as at night. True or False? Cross your answer.

TRUE   FALSE

194. Tick to show which ones are the duties of a good citizen.

A. Throwing trash in bin
B. Casting vote
C. Helping the elderly
D. Getting into a fight

195. Circle the heaviest animal on land.

196. Change **daisy** to its plural form. Circle the correct answer.

a) daisies   b) daisys

c) daisers   d) daisy's

197. Which shape has the maximum area? Tick the right option.

A. Blue

B. Red

C. Yellow

D. Green

198. Circle the objects that can make sound.

199. Which of the following is the planet closest to the sun? Cross your answer.

Earth

Mercury

Saturn

Venus

200. Did you know? Swans remember who has been or not been kind to them! Complete this picture of a swan.

201. Circle the bird that does not build its own nest and lays eggs in a crow's nest.

202. Which of these units is used to measure quantity of gases?

1. gram
2. litre
3. metre
4. hour

203. Will the candle continue burning for long in this closed case? Circle your answer.

YES

NO

204. Circle the colour that is warm.

a) red   b) blue   c) green   d) pink

205. If the length and breadth of this rectangle are 8 cm and 3 cm respectively, what will be its perimeter (sum of all the sides)? Tick the right answer.

8cm
3cm

21 cm   20 cm   11 cm   22 cm

206. If you sleep from 10 pm to 7 am, how many hours would you have slept in 4 days? Circle your answer.

48 hours   36 hours

32 hours   27 hours

207. Circle the object that has one syllable in its name.

208. Circle that which the tree has in the largest number.

209. Which colour of the traffic lights means 'get ready'? Tick the right colour.

a) Red

b) Green

c) Yellow

210. Circle the units of temperature.

a. Celsius

b. Degree

c. Fahrenheit

d. Numbers

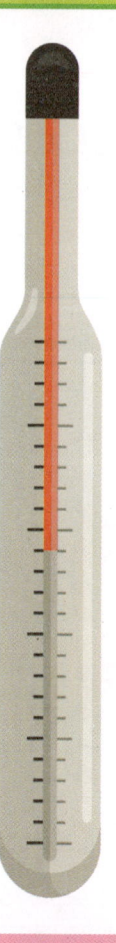

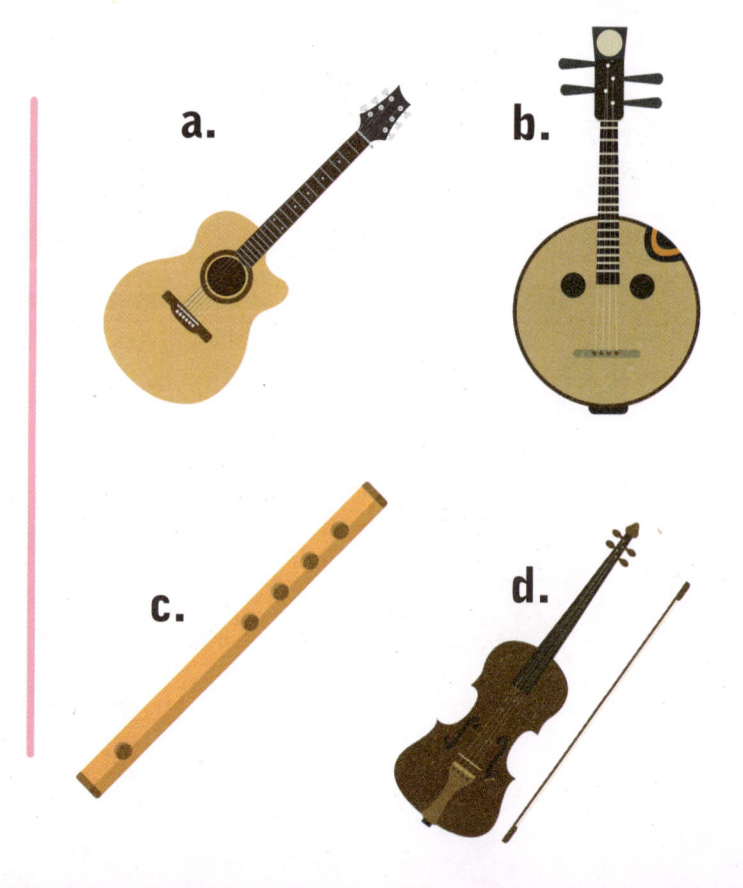

211. Circle the banjo.

a.

b.

c.

d.

212. What is the quotient when you divide the sum of numbers in red blocks by the number in the green block? Tick the answer.

14
8 9
7 4
3 2

A) 4   B) 5   C) 1   D) 6

213. What is the maximum portion of the earth covered by? Circle the right answer.

a) Land
b) Water
c) Lava
d) Trees

214. What is the process of sprouting of a seedling from a seed called? Circle it.

a) germination   b) growth
c) birth   d) germicide

215. What is the process of gathering in the crops from the field called? Complete the word to answer.

H _ _ V _ _ T

216. Tick the correct **homophone** (same sounding word).

- tail
- tale

217. Circle to show that which is the same as 1 + 4.

a) 4 + 7

b) 3 + 2

c) 6 − 1

d) 7 − 2

218. Circle the **renewable** (which will never get over) resource.

219. Which country is called Nippon, or the 'land of the rising sun'? Cross the right answer.

a) China

b) India

c) Egypt

d) Japan

220. Count in 7s and circle the correct answer.

a. 21   b. 42

c. 35   d. 31

221. What gives colour to the skin of human beings? Write in the boxes below.

M _ L _ N _ N

222. How many cubes would have made this structure? Cross the right answer.

a) 5   b) 7   c) 9   d) 11

223. Number the stages of the lifecycle of a butterfly as they happen.

57

224. What are the rings around Saturn made of? Circle the correct options.

1. asteroids
2. satellites
3. meteors
4. comets

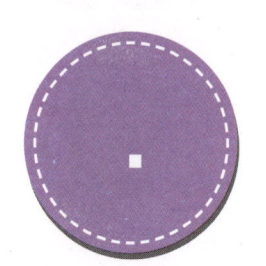

225. Solve this puzzle by filling in the blanks with numbers or mathematical signs.

a. ___	x	2	12
x		x	
3		b. ___	
18	c. ___	8	d. ___

226. Place the correct punctuation mark in the blank.

Tomorrow is the last day of the festival ____

? . ! ,

227. What is the difference between the numbers of jellybeans in the two jars? Tick the answer.

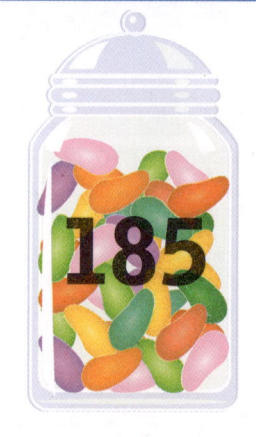

185   135

a) 40   b) 50

c) 60   d) 30

228. Who will win if there is a race amongst them? Circle your answer.

229. Jerry obeys his elders and speaks politely with everyone. He also shares his candies and toys. He is _____.

a. disciplined

b. naughty

c. well-behaved

d. arrogant

230. Can you draw four lines using these dots?

231. Tick in the shapes in which you cannot draw a diagonal line.

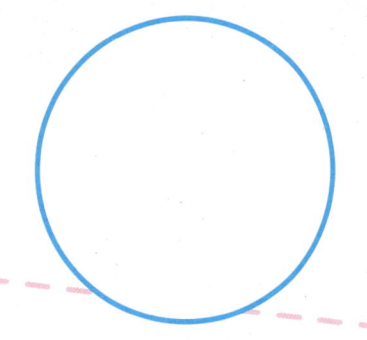

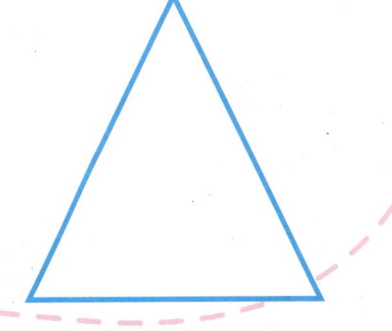

59

232. Which number is repeated the most in this table? Tick the answer.

4	3	2	1
8	2	6	4
9	7	4	1
4	6	9	7

a) 4   b) 2
c) 6   d) 7

233. Which one is the prey in this picture? Circle and show.

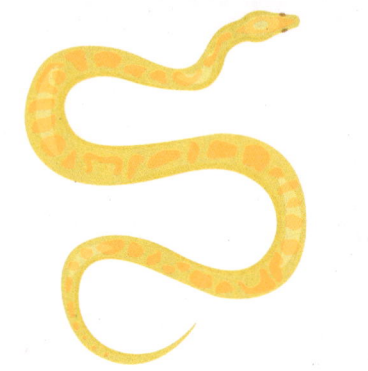

a) Snake

b) Frog

234. Circle the picture to show the one who decides punishment for a criminal.

235. Draw what comes next in the two patterns.

A

B

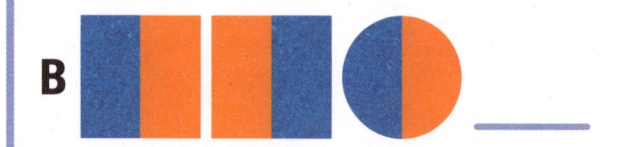

236. Circle the sentence.

a) I like to eat mangoes.

b) mangoes and strawberries.

c) He is playing with toys,

d) tomatoes and oranges.

237. Which is the longest? Circle your answer.

238. Circle the body part that helps you to stand straight.

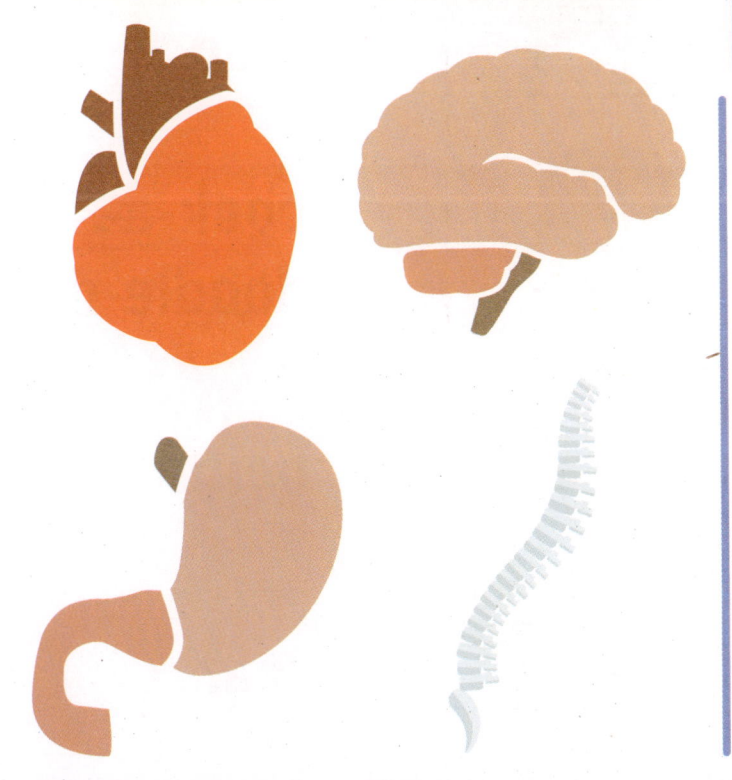

239. What is the part of a bicycle that the arrow is pointing to called? Fill in the blanks to answer.

S _ _ _ E S

61

240. Circle the shadow of an eagle.

241. Rewrite the jumbled letters to name the animal in the picture.

C O U I N N R = _____

242. How long would be the leaf? Tick the right option.

a) 5 miles

b) 5 inches

c) 5 yards

d) 5 litres

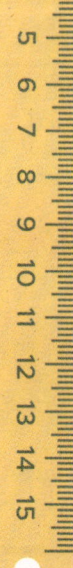

243. Match each animal with its sound.

moo

cock-a-doodle-doo

neigh

roar

244. Cross off the beings that are imaginary.

245. If you are born on this date, your birthday will come every 4 years. What date is it?

LEAP YEAR
366

a. 28th February   b. 30th April

c. 29th February   d. 31st March

246. Match the pictures that are called the same.

247. What is the fraction of the empty glasses? Cross the right fraction.

$4/5$ $5/10$ $3/5$ $4/10$

248. Match each state of matter with the arrangement of molecules in it.

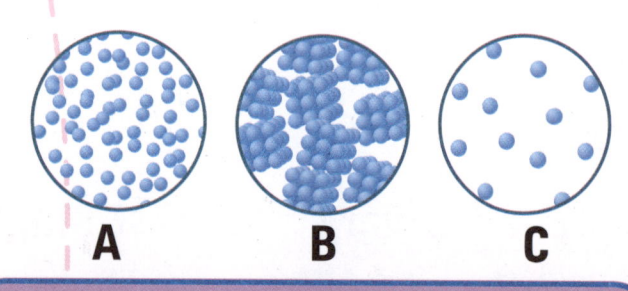

GAS   LIQUID   SOLID

A   B   C

249. Cross the words with incorrect spellings.

friend

sattelite

recieve

cosy

jewellry

250. Write the words in the table as per their category.

| ful | dis | un |
| ment | non | ness |

Prefix	Suffix

251. Circle the object you use to find the meaning of a word you do not know.

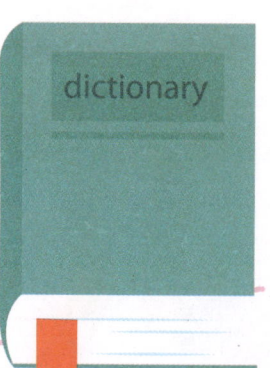

252. 13578 > 13576

Tick the right answer.

TRUE

FALSE

253. Match each gemstone with its name.

- sapphire
- amethyst
- ruby
- emerald
- diamond

254. Circle the currency used in Europe.

$ ¥ £ €

255. Help the honey bee reach its hive.

256. Look forward, backward, vertically and diagonally to find the 5 animal names in the word search.

O	M	U	U	R	A	W	R	P	E
H	O	R	S	E	F	W	M	H	L
Q	O	B	P	R	E	G	I	T	E
Y	T	I	W	I	A	I	B	B	P
W	U	V	L	P	M	B	B	Q	H
C	R	O	C	O	D	I	L	E	A
N	B	W	N	R	F	G	B	R	N
R	R	E	L	P	C	G	Q	V	T
H	E	E	A	P	R	G	S	Q	C
Y	O	G	A	R	K	L	I	Y	R

257. Jenny has $20 in her money box. Jude has $35 in his money box. How many more dollars does Jenny need to have the same as Jude?

a. 10
b. 15
c. 20
d. 25

258. Circle the picture of the object that should always be used while doing an experiment.

259. If a clock's circumference is 15 inches, how many inches does its hour hand cover in one day? Cross the answer.

A. 35 inches

B. 30 inches

C. 60 inches

D. 15 inches

260. Circle the odd one out.

261. What is 'dry ice'? Tick the answer.

a) solid carbon dioxide

b) carbon monoxide

c) frozen hydrogen

d) carbon dioxide

262. There are 1 black, 2 blue, 5 green, 3 red and 4 yellow bricks. How many bricks are there in total? Cross the right answer.

10   15

20   12

263. Circle the t-shirt in which you will feel the hottest during the summer season.

264. Circle the object used to make a house?

265. If in exactly 8 hours it will be the next day, what time is it right now as per the 12-hour clock? Tick the right answer.

2:00 pm

6:00 pm

12 noon

4:00 pm

266. Cross the other word for **a bad dream**.

dangerous   nightmare   scary   story

267. Find and circle at least 6 differences.

268. How are clouds formed? Tick the correct answer.

☐ a) By the evaporation of water from the seas

☐ b) By boiling water in a pot

☐ c) By throwing water in the air

☐ d) By the melting of ice

269. Which ball is used to play golf? Circle the right answer.

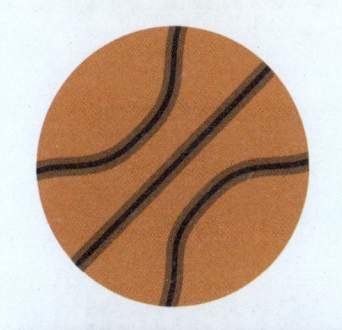

270. How many blocks are covered by the red heart? Circle the right number.

10   15   12   14

271. What is the root word for actor (for example, root word for slower is slow)? Tick the right word.

acting   acted

action   act

272. Circle the option that shows the longest line segment.

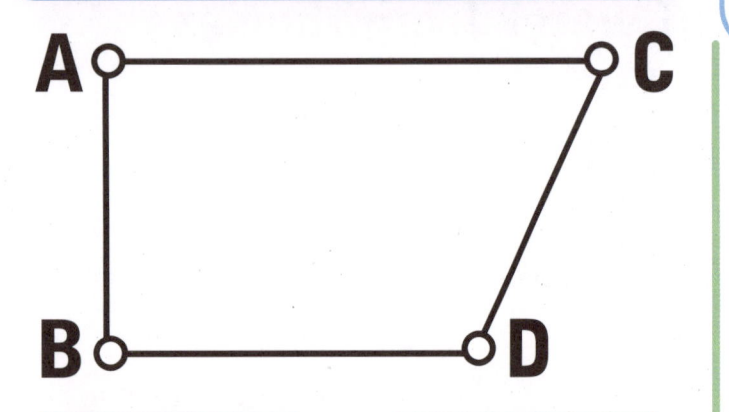

A □——————□ C
 | \
 | \
B □————————□ D

- A to B
- B to D
- A to C
- C to D

273. The arrow is pointing to the _____ in the compass. Cross the answer.

- South 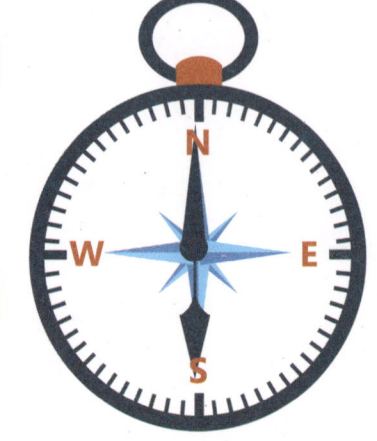
- North
- East
- West

274. Circle the habits that can get you in trouble.

- Lying
- Obeying
- Singing
- Stealing

275. Write the position (ordinal number) of the following letters in words. The first one is done for you.

G - seventh

K - _____

L - _____

T - _____

W - _____

X - _____

276. Write the comparative and superlative forms of 'far'.

          Comparative   Superlative

far   _____   _____

277. What fraction of the circle is coloured in blue?

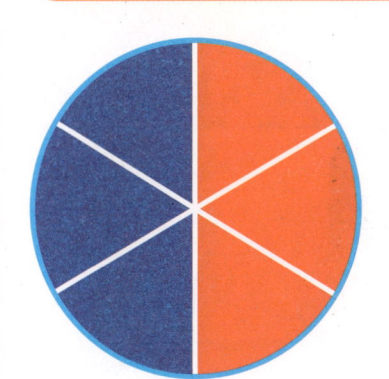

2/4   3/4   2/6   1/2

278. Who treats sick animals? Tick the correct answer.

Dentist   Postman   Nurse   Veterinarian

279. Circle the reptiles.

280. Which animal is on the left side of the box? Tick the right answer.

1. Donkey ◯   2. Cow ◯   3. Lion ◯   4. Dog ◯

281. Circle the consonants in the word.

CONSONANTS

282. What should you take when you have a fever? Circle your answer.

283. Circle the animal that is cold blooded.

284. Complete the picture of the national bird of the USA.

285. Which sentence should come first? Tick your answer.

My name is Whitney. ☐

What is your name? ☐

Nice to meet you, Whitney ☐

Good night ☐

286. Cross the conjunctions.

and, but, or, yet, so, because, being, is

287. What would you do if a stranger came and gave you a candy? Tick the right answer.

- You will take the candy.
- You will not take the candy.

288. When you inhale (breathe in) and exhale (breathe out) air, you _____.

breath | breathe
smell | broth

289. Circle the picture that is facing the same direction as this picture:

290. Add the last-but-one and last-but-two numbers and write the sum.

| 16 | 15 | 14 | 13 | 17 |

291. Circle the animals that are not a reptile.

292. What did the Stone Age man first use to light fire? Circle the object.

293. Colour this picture with only secondary colours.

294. Circle the picture that shows the opposite of 'silent'.

295. How likely are you to find a treasure chest in your garden? Tick the correct answer.

More likely ☐

Less likely ☐

296. Match the moods with the colours they are associated with.

anger	pink
jealousy	blue
sadness	red
blush	orange
energetic	green

297. Circle the face that is 'gloomy'.

298. Cross the words that can mostly be used in the place of 'so'.

therefore

thus

hence

because

as

though

299. Circle the seventh number from the right in the sequence.

9 8 7 6 5 4 3 2 1

300. Cross the consumer in this picture.

301. Tick the statement whose value would be equal to 100 + 40 + 2.

50 + 50 + 42 ○

60 + 40 + 2 ○

100 + 20 + 4 ○

200 + 20 + 2 ○

302. Which shape is the pencil about to draw? Tick and show.

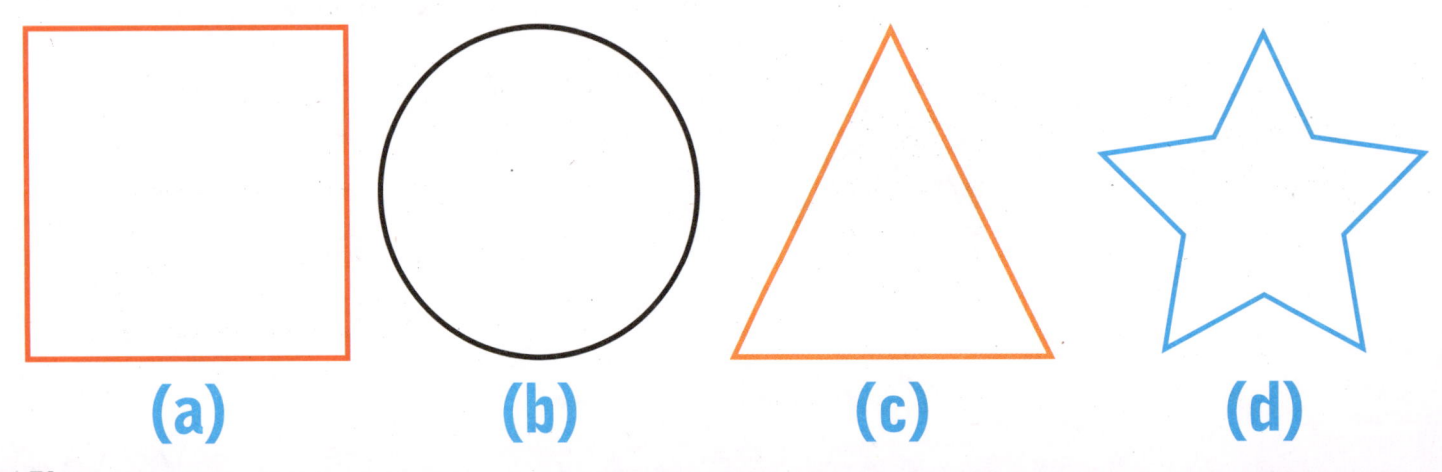

(a) (b) (c) (d)

303. Circle the picture that has two syllables in the word.

304. Tick the **odd** number.

120   246

237   468

305. _____ are solid things found in the nature, made up of minerals.

Circle the correct option to complete the statement.

a) Bodies of water   b) Rocks

c) Piles of soil   d) Pieces of wood

306. Circle the picture that wastes electrical energy.

307. Which of these items is heavier? Cross the answer.

○ Cotton   ○ Magnet

○ They both have the same weight.

308. Circle the verb(s).

anger   playing

america   happily

309. Write the numbers in the correct order, from lowest to highest.

2100   1999   2000   1800

= _____

310. Colour the stem vegetables GREEN and root vegetables RED.

Carrot    Onion 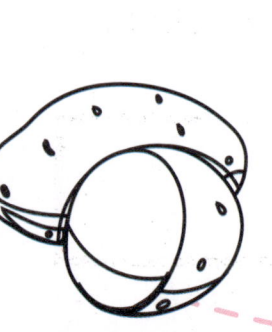   Potato 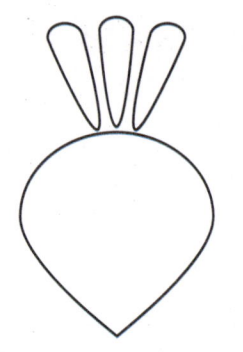   Turnip

311. Circle the object that uses a fuel to function.

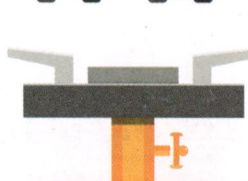

312. Which shape comes next?

A B C D

313. An adjective is the name of a person, place or thing. Tick the right answer.

TRUE

FALSE

314. Circle the 'parallel' sides.

315. What would happen if water is kept at a very low temperature, like -30°C? Cross the answer.

○ **A** It will freeze.

○ **B** It will become lava.

○ **C** It will remain the same.

○ **D** It will become steam.

316. Circle the thing(s) that can harm your eyesight if you look at them for too long.

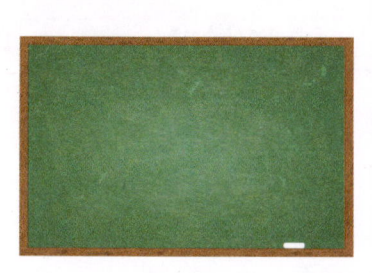

317. Can you tell whose shape is this? Tick it.

dog ○
rabbit ○
horse ○
cat ○

318. Can you find these words?

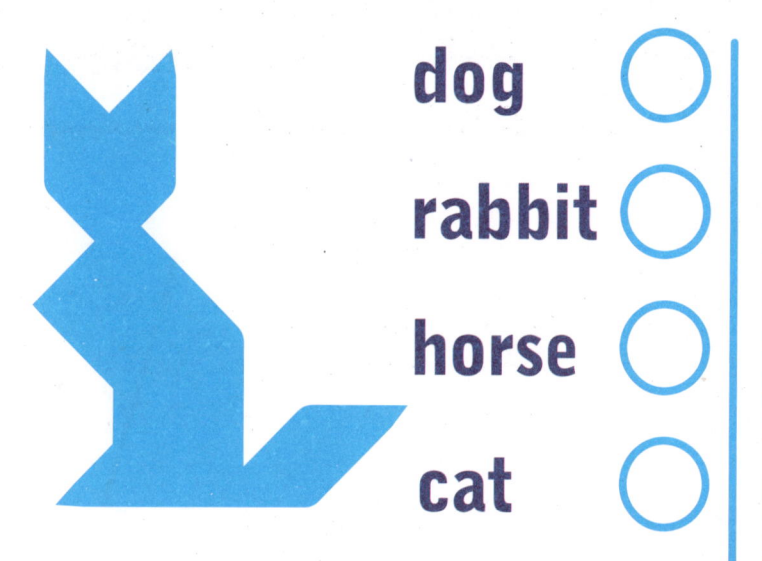

FOREVER, TODAY, TOMORROW, YESTERDAY

O	I	O	I	C	E	X	Y	P	Y
U	Z	P	T	D	T	O	D	A	Y
V	K	W	O	R	R	O	M	O	T
V	H	N	Q	X	J	R	N	M	M
E	W	K	C	L	E	Y	L	U	Y
S	T	C	J	V	B	G	U	X	U
T	M	M	E	F	A	H	R	P	D
L	E	R	V	B	I	G	B	U	F
K	O	S	T	E	D	M	B	W	L
F	Y	A	D	R	E	T	S	E	Y

319. Circle the digit that is at the highest place in this number.

2019 → 2 0 1 9

320. Circle the things that most likely do not have life anymore.

321. What is the **easiest** mode of transportation?

322. Solve this Sudoku.

5	8		3	1	9			
	1		8				3	7
9							1	8
6	2				8		9	4
	9			5				
		8		9	6		1	3
	7	5			1		3	
			5		7	8	4	
1		2			3		5	

323. What do you say if someone sneezes? Tick your answer.

A) Thank you!

B) Sorry!

C) Get out!

D) God bless you!

324. Can you see a 3D shape here? Write YES or NO in the box.

325. Circle the animal(s) whose young one is called calf.

326. What colour do you get when you mix yellow and blue?

red   green   orange   purple

327. Circle the vehicle(s) with headlights.

328. Any story that is the imagination of the writer, without true facts, is called a _____.
Circle the right answer.

non-fiction   fiction   legend   play

329. Fill in the numbers missing in the pattern.

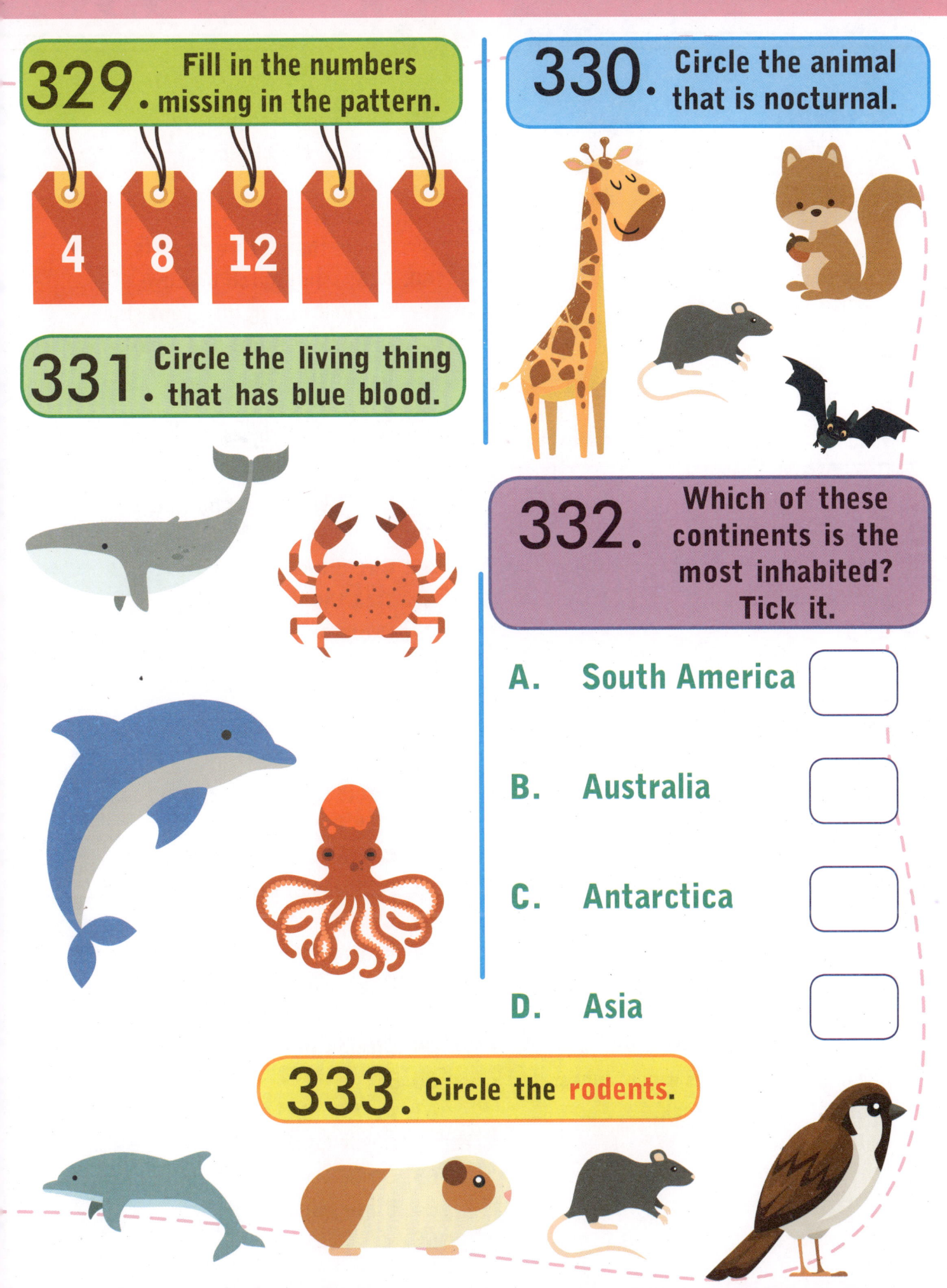

4, 8, 12, ___, ___

330. Circle the animal that is nocturnal.

331. Circle the living thing that has blue blood.

332. Which of these continents is the most inhabited? Tick it.

A. South America ☐

B. Australia ☐

C. Antarctica ☐

D. Asia ☐

333. Circle the **rodents**.

ANSWERS

1. Tick TRUE.
2. Circle the pink one.
3. Tick the skiing child.
4. cold
5. large
6. Draw smaller hand pointing at 12 and larger hand pointing at 7.
7. living
8. Tick PLUM.
9. a
10. The
11. Circle frog.
12. Cross off black.
13. Jane scored higher than Sam.
14. Draw a line crossing the middle of the picture of Earth.
15. 2
16. Circle the first picture.
17. 1. and 3.
18. Wow, we did it!
19. 6, 3, 5, 4, 2, 1
20. Circle the last bird.
21. Circle the second picture in the first column.
22. D.
23. Cross off dog.
24. a)
25. Circle the pupa.
26. Cross off the turnip.
27. Tick Sun.
28. sixth
29. Circle all the pictures except lungs.
30. Cross off the red block.
31. Colour the dolphin.
32. a
33. 13
34. Match liver to digestive, lungs to respiratory, kidneys to excretory and bone to skeletal.
35. Circle the last picture.
36. Tick all the choices.
37. a and c
38. Circle STEM.
39. Circle the picture of cells.
40. A. Missing patch on cow
    B. Duck facing different side
    C. Duck without one wing
    D. Rabbit's face
    E. Sheep's tail
41. thought, was, beat, woke, burst, forbade
42. Tick d.
43. Circle whale and dolphin.
44. Tick 365 days.
45. Circle the star shape.
46. Tick the first picture.
47. Cross off ultraviolet.
48. Circle books and ball.
49. South-East
50. Cross off moon.
51. Circle the first boy.
52. Circle the first shape.
53. Tick CHEST.
54. Circle potato and corn.
55. Pictures are to be completed.
56. C.
57. A: atmosphere; B: hydrosphere; C: lithosphere; D: biosphere
58. CHLOROPHYLL
59. Circle fan.
60. 3.
61. A. 7,0   B. 5,6   C. 0   D. 11
62. Circle bear.
63. Circle the boy pulling the box.
64. Circle the turnip.
65. a.
66. semi-circle

67. cuboid
68. Tick a and d.
69. Tick - plane, deer, right, two
70. 2/4
71. TRUNK
72. H_2O, CO_2, O_2, O_3
73. Cone and cube
74. Tick A.
75. 100, 1000, 1000, 8, 1000
76. Bedrock
77. Australia
78. Eel
79. b) and c)
80. 3, 16
81. Tick FALSE.
82. a. Evaporation b. Condensation c. Precipitation
83. Tick TRUE.
84. C.
85. 10, 20, 30
86. go, need, wants, wish
87. Cross off Taj Mahal.
88. Adverb of place and Adverb of manner
89. Circle the rabbit.
90. Tick 4 - 2 of man and 2 of watch
91. Circle ox, horse and donkey.
92. 100 + 25; 150 - 25
93. Connect the dots to complete the elephant.
94. Tick d.
95. Circle tree.
96. Cross off Pluto.
97. Cross off the child watching TV.
98. Tick b.
99. Tick 7.
100. Cross off the louse.
101. Circle airplane.
102. Tick a.
103. Tick NO.
104. 7:45 pm, 2:20 pm, 4:35 pm
105. Circle the glasses, trousers and scissors.
106. Tick B.
107. Tick D.
108. Circle C.
109. Tick $36.
110. Tick A.
111. Circle wood and water.
112. Circle the water bottle.
113. Cr
114. Circle a.
115. Circle the pine tree.
116. Tick B.
117. Circle 15.
118. Tick a.
119. Circle 11.
120. Circle the diamond, wood and building blocks.
121. Circle the dinosaur skeleton and mummy casket.
122. Tick 1.
123. Mosquito - left to right, first row. Butterfly - left to right, last row. Lizard - left to right, third row. Honeybee - top to bottom, second column
124. A. < B. > C. = D. =
125. Cross off ostrich.
126. Circle Jupiter.
127. Cross off the circle.
128. CONTINENTS
129. Tick A.
130. Circle cheetah.
131. Circle YES.
132. Tick B.
133. 1. Opinion; 2. Fact
134. Cross off C and D.
135. vibrations
136. Tropic of Cancer
137. Circle the second boy.
138. Cross off the gloves and slippers.

139. Draw a line from the cube to 6.
140. Cross off lungs.
141. Tick TRUE.
142. Circle C.
143. Friction
144. Circle 2.
145. lava
146. Tick D.
147. Circle Ears.
148. i. Circle A,E   ii. Circle E,E,A
    iii. Circle U,E,A   iv. Circle A,A,A,O
    Vowel not used - I
149. Cross off O.
150. Circle dog.
151. Cross off Aluminium.
152. Circle A.
153. Circle Neptune.
154. Circle rectangle.
155. Circle owl.
156. Tick D.
157. Circle A.
158. A. s B. es C. s D. es
159. Tick C.
160. Tick the picture of forest.
161. Brushing your teeth
162. 550 cm
163. Join the dots from 5 to 95 to complete the picture of pumpkin.
164. Tick B.
165. Circle the glass of milk.
166. Tick D.
167. school, swarm
168. Circle b.
169. Cross off A.
170. Circle Clouds.
171. Trace the path leading to the apple.
172. Tick B.
173. Tick a.
174. Tick A.
175. Tick B.
176. Circle FALSE.
177. Circle B.
178. Circle spinach and carrot.
179. Tick B.
180.

9	6	4	3	2	7	8	1	5
2	1	7	9	8	5	6	4	3
3	8	5	4	6	1	9	2	7
6	3	1	7	9	2	4	5	8
5	9	8	1	4	3	2	7	6
4	7	2	6	5	8	1	3	9
7	4	9	2	3	6	5	8	1
1	5	6	8	7	4	3	9	2
8	2	3	5	1	9	7	6	4

181. Tick B.
182. Tick B.
183. Circle the first picture.
184. Circle burger and fries.
185. Cross off the paint can.
186. A. un B. dis C. un D. dis
187. Circle 15.00
188. Circle ant hill.
189. Tick TRUE.
190. Circle hen and rabbit.
191. Write 'a'.
192. Tick D.
193. Cross off FALSE.
194. Tick A., B. and C.
195. Circle elephant.
196. Circle a.
197. Tick C.
198. Circle pot and can.
199. Cross off Mercury.
200. Complete the other half of the drawing to make a swan.
201. Circle the picture of cuckoo.
202. litre
203. No
204. Circle red.
205. Tick 22 cm.
206. Circle 36 hours.
207. Circle kite.

208. Circle leaf.
209. Tick c.
210. Circle a and c.
211. Circle b.
212. Tick B.
213. Circle b.
214. Circle a.
215. HARVEST
216. Tick tail.
217. Circle b, c and d.
218. Circle the sun.
219. Cross off d.
220. Circle a.
221. MELANIN
222. Cross off c.
223. eggs:1 caterpillar:2 cocoon:3 butterfly:4
224. Circle 1 and 4.
225. a. 6 b. 4 c. - d. 10
226. full stop (.)
227. Tick b.
228. Circle cheetah.
229. well-behaved
230. Connect dots, except for the middle dots up and down.
231. Circle and triangle
232. Tick a.
233. Circle b.
234. Circle the first image.
235. A. Repeat the same square as before.
     B. Add the mirror image of the circle.
236. Circle a.
237. Circle third option.
238. Circle the last image, of spine.
239. SPOKES
240. Circle the second shadow.
241. UNICORN.
242. Tick b.
243. Match horse: neigh, lion: roar, rooster: cock-a-doodle-do, cow: moo.
244. Cross off the unicorn, dragon and alien.
245. 29th February
246. Draw a line between the red bow tie and the bow.
247. Cross off 4/10.
248. A: LIQUID, B: SOLID, C: GAS
249. Cross off b, c and e.
250. Prefix: dis, un, non
     Suffix: ful, ment, ness
251. Circle dictionary.
252. Tick TRUE.
253. red:ruby; blue:sapphire; green:emerald; white:diamond; purple:amethyst
254. Circle the last picture.
255. Trace the path from the bee to the hive.
256. Across: (L-R) Horse, Crocodile; (R-L) Tiger
     Down: Elephant; Diagonal: Bear
257. $15
258. Circle goggles.
259. Cross off B. (15 x 2 = 30)
260. Circle boy with book.
261. Tick a.
262. Cross off 15.
263. Circle the black t-shirt.
264. Circle brick.
265. Tick 4:00 pm.
266. Cross off 'nightmare'.
267. 1. colour of butterfly
     2. direction of the grasshopper
     3. fly on the tree
     4. mouth of the caterpillar
     5. design on the spider's body
     6. hands of the ant
268. Tick a.
269. Circle last ball.
270. Circle 10.
271. Tick act.
272. Circle A to C.

273. Cross off South.
274. Circle Lying and Stealing.
275. K - eleventh; L - twelfth; T - twentieth; W - twenty-third; X - twenty-fourth
276. farther, farthest
277. ½.
278. Tick veterinarian.
279. Circle crocodile, dinosaur and tortoise.
280. Tick cow.
281. Circle C,N,S,N,N,T,S.
282. Circle medicines.
283. Circle fish.
284. Complete the picture of eagle.
285. Tick 'What is your name?'
286. Cross off all the words except 'is' and 'being'.
287. Tick 'You will not take the candy'.
288. breathe
289. Circle lion.
290. 27
291. Circle frog and fish.
292. Circle stones.
293. Colour the picture in any colour except red, blue and yellow.
294. Circle the first picture.
295. Tick 'Less likely'.
296. anger:red; jealousy:green; sadness:blue; blush:pink; energetic:orange
297. Circle the last picture.
298. therefore, thus, hence
299. Circle 7.
300. Cross off giraffe.
301. Tick the first sum.
302. Tick b.
303. Circle 7.
304. Tick 237.
305. Circle b.
306. Circle the second picture.
307. Cross off 'They both have the same weight.'
308. Circle playing.
309. 1800, 1999, 2000, 2100.
310. Stem vegetables: potato and onion
     Root vegetables: carrot and turnip
311. Circle the gas stove.
312. D
313. Tick FALSE.
314. Circle AB and CD.
315. Cross off A.
316. Circle computer and mobile phone.
317. Tick cat.
318.

O	I	O	I	C	E	X	Y	P	Y
U	Z	P	T	D	T	O	D	A	Y
V	K	W	O	R	R	O	M	O	T
V	H	N	Q	X	J	R	N	M	M
E	W	K	C	L	E	Y	L	U	Y
S	T	C	J	V	B	G	U	X	U
T	M	M	E	F	A	H	R	P	D
L	E	R	V	B	I	G	B	U	F
K	O	S	T	E	D	M	B	W	L
F	Y	A	D	R	E	T	S	E	Y

319. Circle 2.
320. Circle the leaf and grapes.
321. Circle bicycle.
322.

5	8	7	3	1	9	4	2	6
2	1	4	8	6	5	3	7	9
9	3	6	2	7	4	1	8	5
6	2	1	7	3	8	5	9	4
4	9	3	1	5	2	7	6	8
7	5	8	4	9	6	2	1	3
8	7	5	6	4	1	9	3	2
3	6	9	5	2	7	8	4	1
1	4	2	9	8	3	6	5	7

323. Tick D.
324. Yes - the jar.
325. Circle cow and elephant.
326. Circle green.
327. Circle scooter, car and truck.
328. Circle fiction.
329. 16, 20
330. Circle bat.
331. Circle octopus.
332. Tick D.
333. Circle guinea pig and mouse.